My Life as a DOG MOM

A Journey of Love, Loss, and Acceptance

POPPY WATERS

Grateful Acknowledgements

Authors Photo: Brook Todd

Book Design: Kyle Ferdinand

Editorial: Carolynne Gamble, Jasmyne Boswell

Front & Back Cover: Anne Keenan Higgins

Illustrations: Anne Keenan Higgins

My Life as a Dog Mom
A Journey of Love, Loss and Acceptance
© POPPY WATERS, 2019

Library of Congress Control Number: 2019915862

ISBN (hardcover): 978-1-7332500-0-9
ISBN (e-book): 978-1-7332500-1-6

1. A Memoir
The events and conversations in this book have been set down to the best of the author's ability, although some names and details may have been changed to protect the privacy of individuals.

All rights reserved. No part of this publication may be reproduced, stored in a retrieval system, or transmitted, in any form or by any means, electronic, mechanical, photocopying, recording or otherwise, without the prior written permission of the author.

Printed in the United States of America.

Dedication

Leia, Harley, Belle, Cisco, Rosie and Kitta. It is an honor to be called your Mom.

Chuck; my best friend and partner for life. I love you with all my heart.

All my mentors, family and friends who supported me during this journey. You know who you are. Thank you with all my heart!

To God and the Universe for supporting, nudging me when I needed it and providing nature to heal me.

To the places I've lived during this journey. Thank you for providing a safe and sacred space to create.

Lastly, to the little girl inside of me, welcome back. This book is also for you. I see you and I love you.

My Life as a Dog Mom

By the time I realized families came in different forms, I had lost mine. It might have helped if, at the time, I had known that I didn't really have complete control over my life. At least then I might have stopped trying so hard for what I wanted so badly, something that seemed to be designed for everyone else but me. But let me backup a bit so you know what I'm talking about.

After admiring each other from afar for ten years, the stars finally aligned for Chuck, an acquaintance introduced by close friends, and me to be together. We dated for eight months and married in 1998. I just knew I loved him, wanted to spend the rest of my life with him, and that was all I needed to know.

We had high hopes for a smooth sailing life and a happy future. And I had good intentions for having a family. In retrospect, those intentions were more like unconscious thoughts or cultural assumptions. Even though we never talked about having children, I used to daydream about putting my kid's school pictures in stylish frames inside the stairwell, so I could see how fast they grew up from K-12.

It wasn't until 2009 that we finally found our forever, perfect home. I knew it was the right one because – you guessed it - it had a large stairwell and a sizeable backyard. It was the kind I'd always dreamed about. Even though the house needed to be gutted and remodeled, it was perfect.

In 2001, when I was in my early 30's, everyone I knew seemed to be having babies, but instead, I had a miscarriage. The women in my life made getting pregnant look easy and effortless. Spread your legs and BOOM, nine months later, a healthy baby pops out. Easy peasy. Family members- babies, close friends- babies, neighbors- babies, colleagues- babies, but not me. Why? Was I meant to be a mother, or was I biologically, physically and/or mentally too screwed up? Did I come into this life to learn the painful lesson of not being able to conceive? Or as it happened, was I to conceive only to experience the emotional mess of mopping up life after miscarrying? I wondered, was Mother Nature going to give me my break? Maybe she accidentally overlooked my name, or for some unknown reason, kept skipping over me. It might sound funny, but it wasn't. The suffering I endured by being childless in a world of mothers chipped away at my heart and hope.

After I miscarried, I threw myself back into my job. I was an outside sales executive with a multi-state territory. Each week I went on the road, traveling to various clients, looking for validation that I still had some self-worth. Unfortunately, my validation in the form of work was short lived. One day while driving to see clients I saw two dogs running on the freeway a few cars ahead of me. A car struck one, and the other fled to safety up an exit ramp. Crying hysterically, shaking, I called 911. That night when I got to my hotel and had time to calm down, I realized something. I wanted to be at home, with my dogs and Chuck, not on the road. I slowly worked up the courage to tell Chuck that I wanted to be a stay-at-home mom. Correction, a stay-at-home dog mom. Was that such a thing? If it wasn't, it was now.

Childless, I felt like a world and cultural rejection, 24/7. I'd go to sleep thinking about having a baby and wake up thinking about having a baby. I'd wonder, maybe deep down I don't really want a baby. My mom used to say, "Having kids will give your legs varicose veins. Make sure you wear support hose when you go to work." At the time I was a 20-year old waitress buying Legg's extra support pantyhose, the kind that came in a giant silver metallic plastic Easter egg container. Was she trying to scare me into not having kids so I didn't get legs that looked like hers? I didn't want varicose veins, but I did want kids, didn't I? Or, did I want children because that's what everyone wanted for me, for us?

No, Chuck and I really wanted a family. It was physically having a baby that scared the shit out of me. Even though Chuck never showed it, I knew he was scared for his own reasons. Sometimes I was so afraid, more like petrified, and asked myself the hard questions, "Am I even fit to be a mother? What if I mess the kid up like I felt my mom messed me up? Was my fear somehow sabotaging me from getting pregnant?"

They say having a baby brings your experience of love to another level, one you can never imagine. Funny, I never heard my mom talk about that kind of love or for that matter, anything else about having babies, except for the varicose vein warning.

I continued to fumble through trying to get pregnant, but in all honesty, at times I didn't put forth too much effort, because it was such a stressful process. Relax, the doctors would say. Just relax. I wanted to scream, "Hey, why don't YOU RELAX!"

Friends and family would ask, "Are you pregnant yet? Are you still trying to get pregnant?" I hated that. They would say, "You know, I heard so and so went to see Dr. Hawker and she got pregnant. You can too, probably." Probably? And there it was, 'probably.'

When I'd think about how hard it was for me to get pregnant, I'd muse, even the Virgin Mary somehow had a baby, so why can't I? Did God deem me unfit? Did he/she have a chart with columns that had my name on the wrong side of the page, like Santa's naughty or nice list? It seemed like just by glancing at a penis some women got pregnant. And other women had kids and didn't even want them. It didn't seem fair.

For 11 years I weaved in and out of the dream of becoming a mom. Eleven years. Eleven long, exhausting, stressful, difficult at times, years. When friends asked the brutal question, I wanted to wipe the pouty look off their faces, as I replied, "Not yet." I wanted to say, "Stop pitying me! It's not helping." Inside I was screaming, "Stop asking!" I felt like a total loser, having to say no, AGAIN. Nothing helped. No amount of sympathy could produce a baby. Little did I know that years later I'd be giving the same head nodding, pouty mouth look back at them as their kids screamed, cried, and kicked. I'd think, Hmmm, maybe I dodged a bullet.

Even so, as years ticked by, I continued to suffer in silence. One doctor told me to only eat organic meat, and I would get pregnant. She said it would help straighten out my hormones. I immediately fired her. One friend told me to sit on my head while having sex to make sure the sperm got to the right places. I ignored her advice.

My latest imagined picture - perfect family looked like this: a husband (check), one son, one daughter and a dog. We'd live in the suburbs, drive a minivan, take the kids to school, pick them up after school, do after school activities, drive to doctor's appointments, have dinner together, help them with their homework, give baths, brush teeth, have story time, wake up the next day and do it all over again. That actually seemed fulfilling to me. My body, however, had other ideas and wouldn't carry a baby to full term.

Friends and family often asked if we considered adoption. We did. They would generalize saying, "Well, I would have adopted if I couldn't have a child of my own." Really? Would you have? How could they be so quick to judge? Have you ever heard anyone passing judgment on people having their own kids, knowing there were orphans and kids in foster homes in need of a family? Have you?

Chuck and I discussed adopting, but in the end it didn't feel right. If it did, we would have pursued it. We talked to people that adopted privately, from their local counties, through various programs in varied ways, but none of those paths felt right for us. When inquiring into other countries, we were either too old to adopt from some or didn't make enough money or have enough in savings for others. And for particular countries, I weighed too much. Yes, that's correct. I weighed too much. Therefore, in their eyes I was "unfit" to be a mother.

Why would I put myself through all of that? Talk about the ultimate judgment. Wow! You're too fat; therefore we won't even consider you. I'm no Angelina Jolie. I get it. But I did have a solid marriage and was willing to give a child a two-parent home. If you look at some of the high-profile cases, famous people are adopting children as single parents. It doesn't make them unfit. I'm just stating a fact. So if I'm thin, then I'm good enough? Or if I'm wealthy, then I'm more fit? Wow. Just wow. Can life be any more in my face screaming you are not enough? Being you ISN'T ENOUGH.

At the age of 40, I was diagnosed with Endometriosis. Endometriosis is a condition where normal tissue that should grow on the inside of your uterus, grows outside the uterus instead. Most of the time it involves your ovaries, fallopian tubes and the tissue that lines the pelvis. It can be painful and chronic. Well that explains the 30 years of excruciating bring me to my knees, periods. Over the years I asked my gynecologists why I was always in so much pain during my menstrual cycle. The answer was always the same; it's just the way your body is designed. I accepted their answers because they were the doctors and supposed to know it all. It wasn't until I decided to see a fertility specialist to figure out what and if anything unusual was happening inside of me reproductively that I learned the truth.

Halleluiah!! I had an answer, finally. I no longer had to feel like an alien and the only woman in the world not able to conceive. I wanted to declare to the entire world, "See, this is why. I have endometriosis; I'm not a total screw up, loser, failure." Now that I had the scientific proof I asked myself, Should I seek out others who had endometriosis? But how would I find them? Stand on a street corner with a sign that says, "If you have endometriosis, please honk." Were there other women like me hiding and suffering? What was I suppose to do next . . .?

My gynecologist, Dr. Zee, said I still had 10 years of baby making left in me. She also said that with the help of science, it wasn't unusual in today's society to have a baby, even at 50. Even though the thought of having a baby at 50 didn't excite me, I was so relieved to hear the news. At the time, 50 seemed old. I didn't want to be a new mother mistaken for the Nana.

The fertility specialist, Dr. Abrahams, suggested I have surgery to remove the endometriosis, informing me that Dr. Zee would perform the surgery. I wasn't exactly jumping up and down at that, but I was willing to try.

I thought, can't I just take a pill or change my diet, pray it away perhaps? She must have read my mind because she quickly assured me that surgery was the only way.

More decisions. I could leave the endometriosis and live with it like I had all these years. Or… I could step out of my comfort zone and take a leap of faith. And let me tell you, from that point on, faith became my life-long friend.

Dr. Abrahams called Dr. Zee and explained my case. I went home, told Chuck the great news and then vigorously researched the Internet's trusted sites. Reading about other people's horror stories and their surgeries scared the 'bajesus' out of me. Some of the stories included every gory detail imaginable. It made me want to slam the lid down on my laptop and run down the street screaming, NOOOOOOOOOOOOOOOOOOOOOOOOOOOOOOOOOO! Wasn't there some sort of 'magic potion' I could take so we could bypass the slicing me open and cleaning me out part? But no, no such luck. Surgery or leaving it alone were my only two options. I had to keep myself calm and centered, haha. In my gut I just knew operating was the right path, our next step to having a baby. Time to get my big girl pants on!

Frankly, I was scared shitless, but wanted to shout with glee about the possibility of my "new" body. The nerve-racking part was that I'd never had surgery. I had a whole mountain of 'What Ifs' dancing around in my head. What if the doctor cuts me open and says, "Eek! This body isn't fit to carry a baby." Or what if after the surgery she said, "Well we got all the endometriosis out, but good luck conceiving."

What if the surgery went perfectly well and I couldn't hide behind my "excuse" anymore? What if in truth, deep down fear had been the real reason I couldn't conceive? What if the surgery was successful, and I still couldn't conceive? I was living in a land of What Ifs.

I also questioned whether or not I would be a good mother. My mom died when I was in my 20's, so I couldn't ask her what to do. I was still afraid I might do to my baby what my mother had done to me. For the record, she wasn't a horrible mother. I know parenting is not easy and she did the best she could. After all, no one is given a failproof handbook on the subject. Too, she'd had a volatile relationship with her own mother. She tried. Growing up she never made huge demands on me and I never really wanted for anything, material wise. But what I did want was a deep bond with her, something she couldn't give. That I did miss.

They say parenting is a natural instinct. Is it? If so, did I have the 'instinct'? Was I up for the task? At last my bottom line fear came to me. If I didn't love myself, or at least didn't feel I knew HOW to love myself, could I love my child? I knew how to take care of myself. Feed myself, bathe myself, go to school, work to make money, etc., but if I had a baby could I love IT when sometimes I wasn't even sure I knew how to love myself?

Those thoughts were embarrassing, and at the core, shameful to admit. Now that they were out in the open, I wondered if that was the real reason I couldn't get pregnant and carry to full term. In the end, even with that realization, I knew I had to trust the Universe. Again, I had to have faith. I still strongly believed that having a baby would lead me down the path of fulfillment and happiness, and the minivan. With that, I would finally have a sense of belonging, a family to love unconditionally and in return, be loved unconditionally. I don't mean to say that the love from Chuck wasn't enough, but you know what I mean. In the end, I just had to stop questioning and at least give the surgery a try.

Remember at the very beginning of my story I said I wished I would have known that sometimes families come in different forms? Well, here it is.

In 1999, soon after we married, Chuck and I got our first dog, Leia.

We came across an adoption event at a nearby pet store. A local rescue group was trying to find homes for Chihuahuas and a chubby Catahoula Leopard puppy named

Leia. For Chuck, it was love at first sight: red hearts floating overhead as if two love birds were staring into each other's eyes, batting their lashes. Leia slept on Chuck's lap the whole car ride home. They were inseparable.

A year later, I saw a puppy in a pet store window while I was making a sales call. It was a female Harlequin Great Dane--the runt of the litter--all ears, big paws and long legs. I went home to talk with Chuck about getting another dog. The store clerk said they were checking her hearing to see if she was deaf. He said she didn't seem to listen. Chuck said either way, we should get her. A few days later the store called to let me know she wasn't deaf and was available for adoption. I rushed back to the store and picked up our sweet puppy. We named her Harley. Within days we realized why the store thought she was deaf. She was just stubborn and always had her own agenda.

A year after that, we were ready to add to our family. I searched the Internet for Great Dane rescues. I found a local group and applied for a few dogs. About a month later I spotted a Dane named Harley (yes, another Harley). She was a one-year-old deaf albino Great Dane. I immediately applied to adopt her.

I met Harley and her foster mom, Nancy, at a park. What a regal Dane she was. On the drive home I decided to change her name to Belle, pending Chuck's approval, of course. The name fit her perfectly.

I couldn't wait to bring her home to meet the rest of the clan. It wasn't love at first sight for our Harley and Belle. Nobody told me sometimes it's not an ideal situation to have two female Danes live together. Committed to making the adoption work, and prepared to make everyone happy, I enrolled Belle in doggie daycare. She was a social butterfly and thrived in that environment.

A few months after we adopted Belle, I received a call that a dog named Cisco needed a new home. He was a sweet natured, handsome, five-year-old mixed breed. He belonged to a friend of the family. They felt Cisco needed more attention than they could give. Four dogs seemed like a lot, but what the heck, why not? The last time I saw Cisco he was temporarily living with the grandparents, because the family was moving into a new house. I suddenly remembered what I had promised Cisco back then: If you ever need a new home, you can come live with us. Little did I know he'd take me up on my offer. Now we had our little man, and he completed our four-pack.

We also had a cat. I would be remiss if I didn't mention Kitta, our female feline. She was a neighborhood cat that showed up on our front porch one fall day, which morphed into banging on the kitchen door at 3:00 a.m., wanting in. She loved to taunt the dogs by walking along the fence, knowing all too well they couldn't reach her. Somehow we made it work, adopting the attitude of what's one more. There's always more love to give. She was/is so sweet, when she wants to be!

I began to see similarities between my life as a dog mom and the lives of my friends who had children. It seemed I was doing many of the same things with my animals as they did with their human kids. I took my 'kids' to the vet (doctor), obedience training (school), drove them to daycare, tended to middle-of-the-night illnesses, got vomited on and pooped on, cleaned up poop and pee from their beds, made sure the other dogs didn't get whatever illness the first two dogs had, paid for pet insurance, picked up prescriptions, sat in photo sessions as they aged, tucked them in at bedtime, kissed them good night, called every day to check on them when traveling, consulted with animal communicators, bathed them, had their teeth cleaned, their nails manicured, kept up with vaccinations, saw to routine health check-ups, scheduled play dates, found the right babysitter, bought their favorite toys and treats, made sure I knew what made them happy and what they didn't like, provided for special dietary needs, celebrated birthdays, took them on vacations, played hide and seek and other games, gave their lives meaning by training them as therapy dogs so they could help kids with reading skills, catered to their specific personality needs, kept them safe and secure, sat with them for pictures with Santa, took professional family photos and took care of their specific issues as they aged.

Am I crazy, or does that sound close to what mothers of human children do? My animals were my life.

Though I didn't give birth to Belle, she was only a year old when we adopted her from a local Great Dane rescue. She was my baby. She was a true Belle, a real beauty. She was a tall, white Great Dane with sky blue eyes and a delicate pink nose. A nose that eventually turned all black as she aged. She was sort of a canine supermodel. Wherever she went, she turned heads. People would always stop us, wanting to meet her. She loved the attention, but not in an arrogant way. She had a huge heart and always, always wanted to say hello. In a sense, she was an Earth Angel. She taught me about love, humanity, and how a simple hello could brighten someone's day.

It is a huge responsibility to raise a dog, let alone a dog that is deaf. And as her mom, I took that responsibility very seriously and with great honor. It was my job as Belle's mom, and of course all four of the dogs, to give them a full life. And because Belle was deaf, getting to know her intimately, personality and all, was key. I had never experienced the level of emotion from any animal as I had with her. When we'd communicate, I/we used sign language. I had to be more tuned in to her, trust my gut and pay attention to her body language. And let me tell you, when she wasn't pleased about something, she'd make her feelings well known by letting out a certain bark that sounded like a seal in distress while her jaw trembled. You hear mothers say, "I know my kid." Well, I knew my kid, Belle. And knowing her, I thought she would make a great therapy dog. So she and I got certified and became a team. But really, it was all about her and for her.

She loved being around people and especially loved kids. We first made rounds at a local veteran's home. Since she was tall and not easy to miss, walking the halls made it easy during our visits for folks to reach out and say hello. Or if we stood in their doorway, she easily got their attention. Some would wave to her and smile, some wanted to tell us about pets they once had and others would just stare. After working with the vets for a while, I thought it might be fun for Belle to switch to the library program, especially since she loved kids. I'm not sure if the reason she loved kids was because she was eye-to-eye with them or just loved their innocence and how they responded with excitement. Or maybe it was all the attention they gave her. The kids would read out loud to her for the purpose of improving their reading skills. They never knew she was deaf. They would show her the pictures in the book, lean on her, kiss and pet her.

It gave me such joy to see how much she loved being with them! I'm sure the parents who watched their kid's reading skills flourish must have felt proud of their accomplishments. It was the same for me. Watching Belle in her element made me so proud and happy for her.

As most parents know first hand, raising a family can be crazy making. That certainly was the case in our home. Having four large dogs definitely kept me busy, 24/7. When one of them became ill, there were sleepless nights, trips to urgent veterinary care, even 3 a.m. feedings.

One particular disaster stands out above all the rest. We'd been living in our new house for about a month. We did the bare minimum to move in, like installing new carpet and a coat of fresh paint. It's all we could afford at the time. We figured we'd renovate over time, as extra funds became available. One day there was a torrential rainstorm, and we realized our garage was going to flood and possibly even our family room. We hurriedly needed to fill sandbags to prevent any flooding. We called some friends for help. I felt it would be best if the dogs stayed in the master bedroom while we were frantically working outside. While filling bags, I heard the dogs barking, but figured they were just excited because they could hear our friends talking and wanted to see them, or perhaps they sensed the urgency in our scurry.

After about an hour or so, we were finished. Whew! Briefly the rain turned into light sprinkles. I ran upstairs to let the dogs outside to go potty. I swung open the bedroom door and could not believe my eyes. Shit Storm. Well, it wasn't just an "expression" in that case. While the storm was happening outside, there was a real life Poop-nado happening in our bedroom. Imagine poop on your bed and brand new carpet. I could see that after one of them pooped, the others stepped in it, parading it all over the room. There was poop smeared on the walls, windows, and doors. The temporary paper blinds were ripped down and shredded.

They even shredded a blanket that was on the bed. To top it off, there was puke on our bed as well. It looked like an official poop and puke crime scene. I'm surprised they didn't write POOP on the windows. And to ask the question who did it? Honestly, they all looked guilty. There were four suspects and their names were Leia, Harley, Belle and Cisco. I wasn't mad. I didn't yell. Honestly, I think I was in shock. My little angels just took pooping to a whole new level. It was a real life poop conspiracy, and our bedroom was the target. I needed a HAZMAT suit or at least head-to-toe protective rain gear. It took several baths, trips to the store and several days to get it all out.

I've heard similar stories about kids taking poop out of their diapers and playing with it in their cribs and smearing it on the walls. But multiply that by four. I could go on, but I think you get the picture!

Even though times like these tried my nerves, taking care of "my kids" who needed me, gave me a sense of purpose. I loved being their mom. Just like human kids, my four-pack loved and thrived by having a routine, breakfast and dinner at the same time every day. On one particular summer day, as is expected, the sun was up early, which meant my kids were up early and wanted their breakfast. They loved when I sprinkled Parmesan cheese on their kibble. So I opened the fridge to get out the cheese only to discover we were out. Ugh! Quickly, thinking on my feet, like moms have to do, I remembered we had packets of Parmesan cheese left over from carry out pizza we recently ordered. Perfect! Or so I thought. By the time I had the packets in hand, three of the dogs had gobbled their food without the added cheese, but not Belle. She was holding out for the extra flavor. I ripped open the packet and sprinkled it on top of her dog food. She looked at it and gave me the look of nope I refuse to eat that. I gave her the hand signal to eat. She still wouldn't eat it. I signaled again. Finally she started eating, but kept looking over her shoulder at me. It was odd. So I took the bowl away and turned on the light. What had I done! Oh my Lord, I sprinkled hot pepper flakes on her food. Shit! That's what I get for not putting my eye glasses on. I immediately called Animal Poison Control. I had the number handy on a magnet on the fridge. I was always a "safety first" mom. The lady that answered the phone asked me to slow down. She couldn't understand me, because I was talking so fast. I was scared the pepper flakes would hurt her. After I calmed down and explained what happened, she laughed. She explained the heat from the pepper flakes doesn't affect dogs the way it does humans, and if we had some milk, that might help her tummy. I gave her some milk along with tons of I'm sorry and added please forgive me kisses. I was mortified. How could I make such a stupid mistake? I felt like the world's worst Mom. Thank goodness she was fine. Whew!!! Dog moms get scared just like kid's moms.

Chuck and I had such fun building memories with the dogs. That's why we took them on vacations, to see Santa and yes, even attended Halloween parades and other activities. Kids love getting dressed up at Halloween and so did my kids.

Two of the four dogs, Belle and Cisco, really enjoyed being in large crowds because they relished the attention.

So every year we dressed them up for the local Halloween pet parade. This particular parade was only a block long. Belle knew how to work a crowd. She would walk a little bit, stop, look around and wait for the crowd to clap and cheer. What a ham! Cisco loved all the attention as well. You could tell by the way he carried himself. If they had given out biscuits instead of the usual candy during Halloween, Cisco would have felt like he'd made it to doggy paradise.

One year, Cisco dressed as a police officer and Belle as a unicorn. Belle won the Judge's Choice award. After the parade, they had a fall festival. Chuck and I walked around, let the dogs have some water, as the sun was blaring on us and checked out the handmade goods at the individual booths. What a fun day. It made me proud to be their mom. Unfortunately, being their mom wasn't all fun and games. Later that evening, Belle was acting a little off, as if she didn't feel well. She didn't want dinner and seemed to have an upset stomach, vomiting and diarrhea. The next morning, Cisco had the same symptoms. We took them to the vet and provided a stool sample from each of them. The results showed they both had coccidia. Coccidia is a single-celled parasite that lives in the wall of the intestine. It can be passed if a dog comes in contact with feces that contain it. This explained their symptoms. Our vet, Dr. B, asked if any of the dogs drank from a bowl of water in public. Yes!! The pet parade! I remember vividly where Belle drank from a bowl. The vet said that if a dog that was carrying it came in contact with water in public, any dog could pick it up. Belle and Cisco had it and this meant the other two would get it. Our house was in a full on, lock down with a strict pill-dosing schedule. We were instructed to give antibiotics several times a day for 10 days. We needed over 200 pills. The vet had to special order the medication for us. It was a high level RED ALERT; full on Defcon 5. Thank goodness they all recovered fine. Its like when kids get lice or chicken pox from other kids at school. There was never a dull moment and always lots and lots of love to go around with them. We were a dog family. Did I already have what I thought I was looking for?

As in any family, you have to take opportunities, regardless of how they interrupt your life. It was no different in ours. Chuck got a job offer that would move us across country, about 2300 miles away. It was an opportunity we could not pass up. The question was how do you move four large dogs, two cars and a whole house that distance? Good question. We decided that moving the dogs via airline wasn't an option. They were too big and frankly, I didn't trust they would be safe in the summer heat. So we rented an RV one-way. We were on a schedule because we had to return the RV by a certain day and time. We made it across country in three days. We made many potty stops and of course, stopped to sleep. Leia was very, very particular of where she went to the bathroom. First day, no potty from Leia, no spots or scent were good enough for her. The second day, every single spot we stopped at, still not good enough to potty. I even went to the extent of leaving the others poop at a certain area at our campsite to see if she would catch the smell and hint. She did not, but another camper scolded me for doing so. I assured her I was on a mission to help one of our dogs. It didn't work. And yes, I picked up the poop.

Now I was getting worried. I said to Chuck on the last morning, "If she doesn't pee or poop, we will have to find a vet. Luckily, that morning during our drive, Chuck spotted a park at one of our stops. Bingo!! Leia LOVED playing ball, especially with Chuck. He decided if he threw the ball enough, she would get distracted and finally go potty. A few throws was all it took. Success!!! Why didn't we think of that first? Ugh. She was fine when we got to our new house late that night. However, to be safe we called a visiting vet the next morning to make sure she was okay, which she was. Keeping them safe and healthy was always of the upmost importance for this dog mom. I was beginning to see how our family resembled other human families. Love is love.

There were so many new beginnings and adjustments we had to make after our move. Some of them were easy, like where to shop, nearby parks, etc. Then there were those that needed research, such as doctors, hairdressers, and of course, in our case, a great vet. So it began.

I've heard my friends talk about how important their relationships are with their pediatricians. It seemed it was the same experience for me when finding the right vet. I didn't think we would be able to replace the outstanding relationship we had with our present vet clinic. Our clinic back east was open seven days a week, included grooming and doggie day care. It was there that we met our pet sitter with whom we would soon become longtime friends. We tried a few different vets in the area, once we moved, and happened upon the Silver's Vet and found Dr. B. Like the old clinic, theirs was a large practice that had several vets to choose from. Dr. B and I just clicked. She was exactly what I was looking for in a relationship with a vet. It just worked, and I was beyond grateful and honestly probably drove her nuts!

When you have children, the rest of your family becomes grandparents, aunts and uncles or cousins. They take an interest in your children's welfare. Parents even contribute to that welfare. Though I was beginning to understand that I already had a family, it was clear others didn't see it that way. One relative asked me what we would do with the dogs once we had kids. That question perplexed me. Another well-to-do relative told me she helped Chuck's brother and his growing family financially, because they had two small children. She claimed she gave them a few hundred dollars here and there. When she told me this, I wanted to yell and say, "Excuse me, just because we don't have human babies, it doesn't mean we don't struggle financially caring for four dogs and a cat – our kids." I thought, really? The nerve. And frankly, I felt insulted. There it was again. The fact that I couldn't have kids was being thrown in my face. We had bills just like Chuck's brother. Vet care, dental cleaning, check ups, illnesses, daycare, pet sitting, food, toys, and grooming. People wouldn't think of giving money to help with a loved one's animal because it's 'just' an animal. This is something that gets overlooked because of the way society views pets. In many households, a pet is a second-class citizen.

It upsets me when I hear pet owner's say, "Well it's JUST a dog. I mean it's getting up there in age and you know, am I really going to pay $2500 for surgery?" If they were talking about their children, it wouldn't even be a question. You made a commitment! Love is love. There's no question in my mind. I feel you do what you can to care for your loved one (human or animal) at every stage of life. When they're a puppy or kitten you can get pet insurance to help pay for their care, even surgery. It cost us $130 a month to cover all four dogs.

Even though the dogs were fulfilling me, I still hoped for a child. Money, money, money, seems like you can do just about anything, if you have it. Well, except MAKE a fertility treatment produce a baby to full term. "When life gives you lemons, make lemonade." Whoever said this should know that doesn't always apply. There would be no lemonade, not yet. I had just finished a fertility treatment that had failed. I felt like I had so many questions as to why with zero answers.

The doctors said, "Try again." My body said, "Um, that's enough and rejected the treatment. My head said, "What the hell just happened?" And my heart sank into my stomach. And if that wasn't enough, now Harley was dying of bone cancer. I started questioning what my life was about?

My world was collapsing around me, and I felt like I was suffocating. I didn't know who I was becoming. I felt like I had failed as a mother all the way around. I was experiencing a tornado of emotions swirling inside of me. I wanted to unzip my skin, peel it off, and hide. I felt trapped and wanted out of this hell. I couldn't save my dog or my baby (the initial miscarriage) and, I couldn't even conceive another one with the help of science. I thought about suicide, but I just couldn't go through with it. That's not me. I stay and fight until the end. Always.

Grief and I weren't strangers. Of course there were items, articles, material stuff I had lost, but this was a different loss. I was experiencing grief compounded by grief. You think it would be old hat to me by now. I'd lost my mom in my 20's, miscarried, and a failed fertility treatment. I thought you have this; you can do this. You're going to be okay, eventually. Just give it time, I kept telling myself. But I didn't have it. The grief of most likely never having a child and Harley's demise was consuming me and my everyday thoughts and moves. I'd wake up and want to go right back to sleep. I wanted it all to be a bad dream. Unfortunately, it was my new reality. Life seemed so unfair.

I just couldn't accept what was happening. Harley was so thin and frail. Her body felt and looked like a bag of bones. We had changed the day and hour of the euthanasia procedure a half dozen times. But as time went on, we couldn't keep doing that to her. Our selfishness was keeping her alive.

She was and had been in so much pain, and now it was our turn. For six weeks we watched her struggle, bounce back and struggle again. It was the bouncing back that played tricks on our minds. I'd say to myself, See, she's getting better. She's doing okay. The truth was she was pooping and peeing on herself and could barely walk. When the vet gave her a big dose of steroids, it was like an adrenaline rush.

She was running up and down the stairs. That gave us false hope, but was short lived. Harley lost her appetite, and in the end we were making food with the blender and feeding her with a large syringe. Whatever she would eat that day, was a victory. Canned dog food, baby food or whatever I picked up at the store that morning. In some ways, like families try to keep a human on life support, we were doing the same with Harley.

I held Harley as the vet administered the euthanasia drugs. I wanted to lay my arm down and yell, "Gimme the juice! I'm going with her." I felt like a part of me was dying. And the truth was, juice or not, a part of me did die that day. As she lay on the bed of blankets we made for her, we let the other dogs Leia, Belle and Cisco, one by one come and say goodbye. After that, Chuck took them for a walk. I sat with the vet, the vet tech, the Reiki practitioner and Harley. I held her and sang, You Are My Sunshine. I have no idea where that came from. I never sang that song to her until that day.

Euthanizing a pet is an agonizing decision. Even though we knew she was in pain. Because Harley was MY baby; it felt like someone had physically reached a hand into my chest and ripped my heart out. When it was done, I looked up at the vet and asked if she was gone. She had tears running down her face and nodded. My baby had crossed over. Her spirit left her body, and now it was just a shell.

Earlier that day Chuck had set up a path through our garage that led to the vet's minivan and covered it in hot pink rose petals from our garden. At the end of the path was a statue of an angel and some of our favorite pictures of Harley. He wanted her to have a grand exit. It was so beautiful. He said it wasn't right to let the neighbors see her getting carried out on a stretcher. It was one of those moments when you say to yourself, oh yeah, this is one of the reasons why I fell in love with him. He's a man and not afraid to be vulnerable and show it. Dr. B said she had never seen anything like it before. I immediately gave Chuck all the credit. I helped carry her body and placed it in the back of the van. I couldn't believe she was gone. What was I going to do now? Who would need me like she did? Is this how mothers feel when they lose a child?

I couldn't stop reminiscing. Even when Harley was 100% healthy, she needed her Mama. She was such a stinker. She would rip the covers off me in the middle of the night and crawl to the foot of the bed because she wanted under to stay warm. One time I woke up and couldn't open up one of my eyes. It was because she had her head on top of mine and her lip was covering my eyeball. Gross, I know. But this was Harley. She was small for a Dane, but full of attitude. When she wanted something, she did everything in her power to get your attention and get her way. She would talk back to me when I would tell her no, and she didn't get her way. When she was outside and wanted in, she figured out how to open the door with her long, banana nose. She was the clown of the four dogs, earning the nickname Boobie. She taught me patience, because she was the one always pushing her luck. If one of the other dogs was in her spot, she would go running to the window, barking frantically to get them to come and see what was outside, then walk away casually taking the spot she wanted. She was no dummy and made no apologies for it. She hated when grandmas would walk by pushing a stroller. They were terribly scary, according to Boobie.

Depression started to creep in. No, actually that's not an accurate description. It was more like depression came to visit and, like an unwanted guest, decided to stay, and it was up to me to figure out how to get rid of it. But getting rid of depression would prove to be tricky. I went to therapy, support group and even sought spiritual advice. Sometimes I couldn't even speak during a session. I would just sit and cry. Like the song from Frozen, I wondered if I could ever "Let it Go, Let it Go." But, in truth I couldn't just let it go and frankly, the depression didn't seem to let me go either. The pain held on like vice grip. No matter how hard I tried to shake it off, it stayed with me. Some days feeding the family and myself were about all I could muster up. Chuck would tell me everyday that things would get better and get back to normal. Most days, I just wanted to stay in bed and sleep the sadness away. Sleeping was my only relief. But each time I did, I'd wake up to the same reality. No baby and now, no Harley.

It was after New Years 2011, and the loss of Harley still weighed heavily on my mind. But I had high hopes that the New Year would give us a clean slate. The relief of starting over was so welcomed. Good riddance 2010! Or so I thought. However, the unraveling of life was still chasing me like a demon I couldn't get away from, grabbing my ankles, trying desperately to take me down. I know they say God will never give you more then you can handle, but I was beginning to break. Like fracture cracks in a structure, it felt like my world was crumbling. Now Leia was dying.

I don't have a lot of memories of what happened, because I was scared and in denial. I was emotionally drained. I couldn't really deal with the grief that was piling up inside. I didn't have anything left to give to Leia— sad, but true. I do remember that she really didn't seem like herself. She'd had an eye removed the year before from an infection and did recover quickly from that. But, when her decline started, there were a series of events that created many downward spiral moments that I can remember vividly.

We had noticed her walking seemed off, so we took her to the vet. They started her on pain meds and told us to watch her. For five pain-staking days we watched her struggle and deteriorate. Dr. B suggested we do an ultrasound. We couldn't believe the results. She had a huge mass on her lung; it covered the whole film. There was no beginning and no end on the image, just the mass itself. Leia had lung cancer. I don't even remember how long she said she might live. I just know she was too far along to try and do anything like chemo. So we waited. By the weekend nothing had really changed except she wasn't sleeping, which meant we weren't sleeping. So we took shifts laying on the floor next to her in the family room, so we could be near the back door to let her out quickly when needed.

I remember her body started getting stiff. First the front end, then that would ease up, then the back end. She would cry on and off. She was always our sensitive girl when it came to her hindquarters. Poor thing was born with bad hips. So the whining didn't concern me a whole lot in terms of her being in pain, except when it went on all night. The next morning we took her back to the vet and they upped the pain meds. She was walking, but looked very wired. Thinking back, I know that was the look of major pain and organs shutting down. By Monday morning we loaded her into the back of our van to go back to the vet. I asked Chuck to take her and Dr. B would monitor her for the day and give her fluids. I knew in my gut when I covered her up and kissed her goodbye that she was dying. I called a couple of times that morning to see how she was doing, and they said she was comfortable and sleeping. Around 1:00 p.m. I decided to take a shower and go see her. Chuck had a business call and asked that I wait until he was off the phone. Death doesn't wait for phone calls to finish. She died. I got a call from the vet when I was getting dressed. She said Leia had died in her sleep. I knew it. I was so mad at myself for not going sooner. She died alone. I felt like a failure yet again.

    I waited until Chuck got off his call to tell him. He fell to his knees in tears. He too hated that she was alone. I believe that having to euthanize her would have been difficult, because he wouldn't have been able to do it. I would have had to do it by myself. And so, the Universe and Leia made it happen when it was meant to happen. The vet's office left her the way she was, so we could say our last goodbyes. And like that, she too was gone.

    I felt numb. Funny thing was, I was already numb and probably in denial. The crater inside just grew bigger. I really wasn't there for Leia, like I had been for Harley. I was drowning in my own sadness and didn't know how to help myself. I was boggled by the losses. And yet little did I know...

A couple of days after Leia died, Belle bloated. That's when a dog has stomach torsion. It is the second leading killer to dogs, just behind cancer. I couldn't believe this was happening. Luckily, I knew the signs of bloat and called the vet. We ended up at the vet ER and they were able to get the air out and stabilize her. I stayed with her until the middle of the night and decided if she was coming home the next day, I'd better get some sleep. I will never forget her lying there, crying. I felt helpless, but beyond grateful they saved her. Maybe life would be calm, for a while. I begged God. I begged the Universe.

That summer, I had a second surgery because the endometriosis grew back. The surgery was a success. At this point I wasn't thinking about having babies, and I was still looking for some down time to get rid of the physical pain.

Bringing new life into the house felt right at this point. So come fall, Chuck and I started entertaining the idea of getting a puppy. Puppies are a lot like babies. You can't let them out of your sight; they need your attention and thrive on schedules. Dr. B said she heard of someone trying to rehome a Harlequin Great Dane puppy. By the time I got the information from her and followed up, they found it a home. So we searched the local rescues and found one that had Catahoula puppies, just like Leia. Chuck was thrilled and we couldn't wait to go meet them. Well, the puppy high didn't last long, because we realized we weren't ready for all that puppy energy. The mother of the puppies, Rosie, was also available for adoption. They asked if we would be willing to foster Rosie. We agreed, but couldn't take her until after the weekend due to a prior commitment. Fostering Rosie would have to wait a couple of days. And the Universe decided to throw us another curve ball, call our bluff perhaps. That same weekend I got a call late at night asking if we were still interested in the Great Dane puppy, Sam, and if we weren't, could we at least foster him. Another foster.

Four dogs and a cat seemed like a déjà vu. We would have our four-pack back. Was the Universe testing me/us? How badly did I miss my babies? Badly. Sam was an emergency foster. The situation where he had been rehomed, turned out to be bad. So we took him in right away.

I made a call the next morning to a woman I knew who lived close by and was very Dane savvy. Both her Danes had died a few months prior. I explained our situation of already committing to fostering Rosie. And to be honest, this poor puppy was a scared little piss ant. She said her house was under construction and couldn't help me. Damn. But as fate would have it, she called the next day and asked if I could bring him over. I talked to Sam and explained to him that he was going to a very nice lady's house and to be a good boy! When we got to her front door, I told him to sit. There he was, acting like a perfect little angel. She flung open the door and exclaimed, with tears rolling down her face that her baby was home. I guess that meant she was keeping Sam. She did, and thank goodness, because I had Rosie to foster and wanted to give her my full attention.

We had fostered a dog many years prior. It was heartbreaking to give it up, even knowing it found its forever home. Having been through it before, I knew I could do it and be fine once Rosie found her forever home. Okay, the truth is, it was a total foster failure. We couldn't give her up. We had her for three weeks and fell madly in love with her. She was such a sweet girl and exhausted from taking care of seven puppies. Her milk had to dry up; she had to get spayed, and then we could legally adopt her. Poor girl slept much of the first three months we had her. I just sort of left her alone and let her acclimate to her new fur family with Belle, Cisco and Kitta.

It's now 2012, about two years after Harley and Leia died. I attended a writing workshop in Hawaii. The organizers planned a whale watch, an activity that tourists enjoy each winter when the whales migrate from Alaska to have their babies in the warm, Hawaiian waters. The morning of the excursion, I meditated before joining the group. I was nervous and excited, so this helped keep me grounded. Harley and Leia spoke to me in my meditation. Leia said, "I'm proud of you." I guess she was proud that I was venturing out of my comfort zone. Frankly, the whole trip was completely out of my zone— a workshop with strangers and the whale-watching trip? Honestly, both scared the hell out of me. Next, Harley came through and said, "Look for me today, I will be with you."

On the way to the boat I shared with my group what came through during my meditation. They seemed uninterested, but listened anyway. We got on the boat and motored a good hour out from shore to see whales. There was Capitan Joe and his two shipmates, Cindy and Megan. I guess their job was to help with the boat and be there if someone got sick or wanted to buy a t-shirt. We were cruising along when Cindy came and tapped me on the shoulder, pointed upward and said, "Hey, see that bird?" There was one bird. One. All the way out in the ocean by itself. I nodded to let her know I saw it. She said, "They call that a Blah Blah bird. I nodded again acting like I heard what she said and smiled. The boat was loud and there were a lot of people talking. I turned back around, looked at Kelly, another writer from our group who was sitting next to me and shrugged my shoulders, as if to say, whatever. Then Cindy tapped me on the shoulder again and said, "Did you hear what I said? I shook my head no. Loudly she said, "That bird is called a BOOBY BIRD." What?? My heart started pounding and my eyes filled with tears.

I said to Kelly, "Oh my God, that's one of my dog's nicknames, Harley, the one dog that came through in meditation that told me to look for her today. Her nickname was Boobie." And there she was, one single bird, flying out in the middle of the ocean. A whole boat of people and Cindy picks me to tell. Coincidence?

When we were done whale watching, our next adventure of the day was flea market shopping and lunch. My voice was hoarse from yelling and cheering with excitement. We saw so many whales and dolphins. We shopped a little and were ready for lunch. While scanning the restaurant menu, I realized they offered Hawaiian rolls with chicken and Swiss cheese. That was Boobie's favorite meal when she was dying. Everyday I would go to the grocery store and buy Hawaiian rolls, chicken and Swiss cheese. She was with me that day, just like she said. I didn't make it up in my head; I heard her tell me clear as day. What a beautiful gift from the Universe. I will forever be grateful.

It was on this trip that it became clear I was done trying to have children. Chuck and I discussed it when I got home and even went to counseling. I told him that I loved him enough to set him free to be with someone who could have them. He said he loved me with or without children. Whew!

And so, The Universe granted me the peace I had been praying for, until the summer of 2012 when Cisco got sick. I pleaded with God, The Universe, please nothing bad, again.

Chuck said he thought he noticed blood when Cisco urinated. We waited until he had to go to the bathroom again and that confirmed it, blood in his urine. It was the weekend so we had to take him to the emergency vet. They confirmed Cisco had a small spot on his kidney. Another dog dying from cancer? The vet said it was rare, and that she only sees this type of cancer maybe twice a year. Since he was a mutt, a very handsome mutt I might add, I figured he would live the longest. He'd been acting normal and we didn't notice anything odd about his behavior or eating habits.

I felt like Cisco had a good life with us. He was 15 years old and was always happy to have his siblings around—loving and accepting. This was his sweet nature. I didn't want to do to him what we had done with Harley, keeping him alive just for our sake. He deserved better. He was still eating, but could barely walk. He lay on the couch most of his last days with signs of pain. I felt awful for him. I even tried acupuncture. We drove an hour each way for an appointment. It seemed to help. I remember sitting with him on the couch, looking at him knowing it was time. I had some soothing music on thinking maybe it would calm and help him pass on his own. I have no idea why I would even think a stupid thought like that, but when a loved one is sick and dying, you grasp for straws.

On his last day, we asked him if he wanted to go for a walk. He got up and waited for us at the door. Chuck wanted to take him, just the guys he said. They went to the end of the block and back. When they came home, he collapsed in the doorway. I knew he wanted to go, and we thought by keeping it normal it might make things easier. The walk was too much. Again, maybe that was for us. Maybe we were both in denial.

We set a time for the vet to come over. This time we lay him in the same spot as we did Harley and made the same bed filled with fresh rose petals. I held him close to me and kept telling him how much we loved him. I sang to him, "You've Got a Friend in Me." I wanted him to remember I would always be there for him right to the end. I wanted it to be over quickly so he didn't have to suffer anymore. Even though he was up there in "dog years" it didn't matter, my heart was broken. The day Cisco died I really tried hard to stay strong for him and be present. I wanted his passing to be as pain free as possible and peaceful. Since we weren't there with Leia when she died, I felt like maybe I could make it up to Cisco by being as present as possible for him. It was so surreal that it was happening yet again. Get me out of this nightmare, I was screaming inside to myself. I yearned for a break, a break as in many long years of no loss, but no, no break, not yet.

On 4th of July, about a week after Cisco died, my brother Frank was admitted to the hospital because of a serious bladder infection. He had been sick for the past 17 years with Lupus, an autoimmune disease, and had been in and out of the hospital a number of times. My dad called and told me something was off "about the infection" and they were running a series of tests. Due to his past, I was not overly concerned. But, when he called again and said that Frank had colon cancer and was admitted to the ICU, I immediately got on a plane to see him and be by his side with my family.

Over the years, knowing how sick he was, we had discussed his mortality often. He asked me if when he died, I would take his two dogs. "Of course," I promised him. I assured him of that again, when he asked from his bed in the ICU. After two and a half weeks of hopes and prayers, his health declined. He was dying. I knew then that it was time to say goodbye, even if he could no longer respond or maybe even hear me. Knowing he would no longer have to suffer, I told him how much I loved him, said goodbye to my family and flew home.

Happy and relieved to be back with my immediate family, I needed to catch up on sleep and ride out my jet lag. A few nights later, Belle fell in the middle of the night. She let out a howl I will never forget. I gave her an anti-inflammatory and sat with her until she went to sleep. I slept on the couch to be near her in case she needed me when she woke up. The next day her leg was swollen. It didn't look normal. Dr. B put a cast on, diagnosing her with a sprain of some sort. But a few days went by and the limping increased. Something was off and I knew it in my gut. A mother knows. We took her in for some tests. A few days later we went back in for the results. The tests confirmed Belle had bone cancer. When the vet delivered the news, I ran out of the room and sat in the van. I couldn't accept it. I wouldn't accept it. I started banging my fists on the steering wheel, screaming, "No, not Belle," pleading with God. You're already taking my brother; please heal Belle. I told Chuck we needed to move the guest room mattress into the family room next to Belle's bed, in case she needed us in the middle of the night. We decorated the corner of the room where she slept with family photos so she could be reminded of how much we loved her.

I remember one night watching her sleep. It was

about 2 am. I started sobbing and holding my chest. My heart physically felt painful and my chest heavy. I knew what this was. This was heartbreak.

Frank died August 22nd the same day we had Belle's cancer-ridden leg removed. Belle died on October 13th. God decided to take them both.

The day Belle died it might as well have been the final nail in my coffin. The image of Belle foaming at the mouth is branded in my mind forever. Dr. B said we could give her as many of the muscle relaxers as we wanted since we were saying goodbye. She could have up to ten pills at once because of her size. We'd never given her more then three at a time. I gave her ten. I couldn't bear watching her suffer. For me, once the decision was made to let her go, I just wanted it over with. No more lingering and hanging on. Make her pain go away.

All the years she gave us filled with love and laughter and her last day on Earth wasn't what I would want for her. It was a Saturday. A crisp fall day. The sky was crystal clear. Two quails appeared in our yard out of nowhere. We had been living in that house for four years and never saw a quail in the yard, not even anywhere on our street. We took it as a sign to trust our wisdom. It really was time to let her go.

After Belle's death, I didn't have it in me to take Frank's dogs. I was beyond emotionally bankrupt and physically exhausted. Thankfully my dad graciously agreed to keep them.

It seemed like after each of our dogs died, we waited a longtime to get their ashes back. Actually, it took about two weeks. But the truth is, I dreaded going to pick them up just as much as I couldn't wait to pick them up. It felt like the healing process really couldn't begin until they were finally back home with our family where they belonged.

We designed a memorial service for each of them based on their personalities. Since Boobie was the "Queen," we left what Chuck had put together for her in the garage - her grand exit - until the ashes came back. When Leia died, Chuck said he wanted to do a private memorial for her while on vacation in Hawaii. For Cisco, we had close family and friends come over and passed around the favorite blue ball that he loved to hump (no joke) while we shared what we loved about him. And finally, for Belle we decorated a Christmas tree in her honor and had friends and family write a special memory on the back of ornaments I made out of photos of her. We chose Christmas because no matter what time of year, she always played with a toy that was Christmas related.

One day, after all the memorials I decided they needed an alter. With the help of a dear friend, we gathered their ashes, collars, favorite toys and photos. We organized them on a bookshelf. When the sun would shine through the window illuminating these treasures, Rosie and Kitta would lay next to it. It's like they knew what it was, and that was their way of honoring their siblings. And then there they were, all my kids, together.

Daily life at this point seemed like a blur. Showering, brushing my teeth, caring for my family as best I could and going to my weekly therapy appointments to cry my eyes out, was what my life consisted of for the next couple of years. I remember vividly one day while doing laundry and cleaning out the lint trap, I found a small ball of lint in my hand. I was dumbfounded. There was barely any pet hair, not like there used to be. I think I was slightly in shock. At my core, I felt like no one really needed me anymore. Yes, I still had Chuck, Rosie and Kitta, but deep inside I felt lost, empty. Was I experiencing some sort of Empty Nest Syndrome? This was my new normal.

By the end of 2013, I endured my third and final endometriosis surgery. In truth, I welcomed the thought of menopause, anything for physical relief. I asked the Universe to go gentle on me whenever menopause came, knowing I'd paid my dues.

I told Chuck I wanted to live near the ocean to heal from the losses. I was afraid that if I didn't, I too would get sick and die. I knew in my gut that I had to do this to save myself. The Saint that he is, he agreed. Thank goodness. At that point I wondered once again, what is the purpose of my life and what do I do with all this pain?

After the move, I cried for three weeks and wanted to go back and tell the people who bought our house to get the hell out. They were living with all of our memories. It didn't seem fair. Did we make a mistake by moving so soon? Was I running away from my feelings?

Poppy Waters

Sleeping in the new house, I had the reoccurring dream. I woke up comforted, confused, happy and sad. I wanted to force myself back to sleep, because this dream felt like home. I'd had this dream at least a half dozen times in past years.

I am back to our old house back East. Someone else owns it and all four of our dogs live there. Of course in the dream, I want to move back in. Like old times, all the dogs are alive and healthy. The touch of their fur, the smell of their breath-it all feels very real. I hug and kiss them all, over and over again. I don't want to let go. Sometimes in the dream our old furniture is there; sometimes I see strangers with the dogs. My old neighbors are there, and I tell them we've moved back in. Once again, I feel complete.

In our new house, while unpacking, I came across an old throw rug. We needed one by the front door, but I didn't want to spend any money right then. The move was expensive. So I put the old rug at the door. It wasn't just any old rug. It was a rug we had at the old house back East. It's a 3 x 5 cream colored (I think it use to be white) shag, fraying at the ends. I can see all four dogs sleeping on it, running or walking on it, even puking on it. It's almost 20-years old. But every time I look at it, it feels like home.

When people came over, they'd probably wonder why I hadn't bought a new one. But the memories and feelings I still get inside every time I walk in and see it are worth their disapproval, if there is any. And now I get to see Rosie and Kitta, laying on it.

Summer is here. I see and hear of kids graduating. Some of them are graduating from kindergarten, some from eighth grade, some from high school and some from college. I am reminded once again of what I don't and won't experience, of what I don't and won't ever have.

But that is looking at the glass half empty. When I look from a different perspective, the glass half full, I see how having had my four precious dogs, I was given the parenting experience even though I didn't fully recognize it the whole time. Being their mom did come natural to me. Like most mothers, I know I made plenty of mistakes, but I did the best I could all along. There would be no graduations, weddings, grandchildren, proms or anyone to carry on the family name. But that's okay.

At the core of it all, however, I did have a loving family unit. There was a lot of laughter, cuddles, kisses, funny moments, adventurous vacations and lots and lots of love.

Learning to accept the hand I was dealt and the choices I made, is something I now accept and am reminded of daily. At times I'm grateful for the way things turned out, and at times I still mourn not having an extended family of human children. It's the ole' the grass is greener on the other side syndrome. There are plusses and minuses to it all. It just depends on how I view it.

I am learning to pay attention and realize what I have in the NOW. I'm not pining for what I think I'm supposed to have or trying to have my life look like everyone else's.

At times I still experience intense grief and sadness that comes out of nowhere, but the reality is that I can't go back. I have to keep moving forward. And I want to keep moving forward, one day at a time, putting one foot in front of the other. My family picture in the end looked different, but in many ways, the result was the same. I am forever grateful and proud to be a dog mom (and cat mom) because at the end of the day, love is love.

Epilogue

Our parents teach us labels. Society teaches us labels. To name a couple, in the early stages girls are to be motherly and play with dolls. Boys become men and are to do the heavy lifting and drive trucks. I know I'm generalizing, but I think you get my drift. Do this by X age and if not, there's something "wrong" with you. It all seems very black and white when in fact it can be very gray. When we live by labels, we leave our truth behind; we live by others' standards. I did this to myself by allowing others' norms to become my own. And when I failed, I felt awful. Not only was I failing myself, first by leaving myself, but in my mind, I failed others as well. I allowed this to happen. As if to say, well "society," I screwed up and didn't live up to YOUR standards. But all along I was lost because I wasn't living by my authentic values. I did what I thought I was supposed to do based on what everybody else did, at least when it came to the idea of what was expected of a married woman. My mom used to say that just because everyone else is doing it, doesn't mean you have to do it. I could have listened better. Dammit, she was right, again.

It was important for me to share my experience of not having children, both the good and the bad. My hope is that it will help others possibly struggling with similar pain, to understand and see that families can and do come in different forms. Life isn't always a Norman Rockwell painting. Sometimes it can look like scribbles on a piece of paper with no beginning or end. My life didn't turn out the way I thought it might, but I've learned to accept the way it has. And, through the pain and the lessons, I'm extremely grateful. From this, I've learned to turn pain into purpose.

Poppy Waters earned her Bachelors of Science degree in Journalism and Graphic Arts and was a featured reporter and writer for her college newspaper. Poppy currently resides in a small seaside town on the West Coast with her husband, dog and cat. She is an animal lover and lives a vegetarian/plant-based lifestyle.

©2019 Poppy Waters. All rights reserved.

www.poppywaters.com

www.ingramcontent.com/pod-product-compliance
Lightning Source LLC
Chambersburg PA
CBHW041956090426
42811CB00014B/1514